Cloverleaf

Cloverleaf

Geer Austin

POETS WEAR PRADA • Hoboken, New Jersey

Cloverleaf

Poets Wear Prada
533 Bloomfield Street, Second Floor
Hoboken, New Jersey 07030
http://pwpbooks.blogspot.com

First North American Publication 2013
First Mass Market Paperback Edition 2013

Grateful acknowledgment is made to the following publications where some of these poems have previously appeared:

Colere, CreamDrops, Mary, The Q Review, Superficial Flesh, THIS Literary Magazine, and the anthology Ganymede Unfinished (Sibling Rivalry Press, 2010).

ISBN-13: 978-0615884776
ISBN-10: 0615884776

Printed in the U.S.A.

Front Cover Image: Roxanne Hoffman
Author Photo: Jonathan Conklin

I have created you in joy and in sorrows:
with so many circumstances, with so many things.

— C. P. CAVAFY

Table of Contents

Cloverleaf

Love Is a Lake

I enter inch by inch.
You lie in the center
of the lake
on a transparent float.
I press my face
to the underside
and watch the movement
of your pink-and-orange swimsuit.
Your belly button winks at me.

Courtship

All these transatlantic phone calls
are beginning to drive me nuts.
What would you say if someone
called you from Paris
and all you heard over the line
was an American rock 'n' roll song?
Friends tell me to ignore the distraction
and get on with work
but I daydream about purple suede boots
silver Lurex pillows and
the curve of you in the palm of my hand.

For M.R.

Everything I do goes into my art,
you said.
You wore electric blue socks
and a black silk ascot.
We sat together in the Café Möhring
on Kurfürstendamm.
I ate a piece of chocolate cake.
You sipped a cup of coffee.
You drew my portrait.
I tried to write a poem.
You said you preferred
to live like a hermit.
Brilliance makes you tick, you said.
We walked in the shadow of the
Kaiser-Wilhelm-Gedächtnis-Kirche.
I asked about Dada and James Joyce.
Ones like myself, you said.
Then we scribbled back and forth
across the Atlantic.
You told me you wanted to suffer.

Ambisexuality

I worshipped masculine Amor
but when Venus in her white leather coat
gray bondage boots
and blond pubic hair came into my bed
I said hello, I love you,
je t'embrasse —
and all that shit.

I thought she'd become my bride
but she got out of bed
and went to a rock 'n' roll show.
I watched her walk down Prince Street
then stumbled to a boy bar
in search of my shadow.

Venus was ivory and gold
up there on her pedestal —
or anyway, white plastic and gilt.
When she tumbled into my arms
I discovered she was made
of softer material —
almost malleable.

Her mouth was red — like a billboard.
Her skin was pale as white.
Her eyes were blue stone.
I couldn't read her face.

Happy Hour

Your eyes are blue
& unfocused in
barroom light.
Your body sits
perpendicular to mine.
You grow toward
the window.

Passage

The time I almost made love to you
was the day before the vernal equinox.

The sun shone vertically on the equator
but its rays angled into your bedroom

where I lay wedged between you and a dog.
On the vernal equinox, you began a trek

ten latitudinal degrees south.
I stayed in New York, where it rained,

and waited for you to inch closer to me
on your journey northward with the sun.

The Smile

You drove me home
and when we got to my place

you smiled a sickly smile that froze me
in my seat for a moment.

I shook your hand, grabbed the door handle
walked into my apartment building, fast

to get away from you.
In the morning I remembered

a smile that was tortured
not shy

a smile that punched through
the patina of your self-esteem.

The Photographer Photographed

You stand on the beach
trying to look like a surfer boy.
You drape your arm across your chest,
your hand rests on your shoulder.
You have a tan
and long black hair.
Your face sprouts
black stubble that glistens in the sun.
You gaze at the camera without blinking
and smile through parted lips.
You look into the eye of the world
and offer yourself up —
a beautiful Damson plum.

Open Heart Surgery

You drop into my life
like a dream of death.
Your lips are blue, and your teeth are cracked.
You puff a cigarette.
Your fingertips glow fiery red.
We go to a bar called The Bar.
You slip away from me and I stare
across the room at ghostlike reflections of myself.
You push past them heading for the exit.
I run after you.
On the street, homeless people
shout political slogans
and groups of the unemployed
try to sell their old clothes.
You dance past them —
your camera flashing at neon signs.
The glare of a streetlamp hits your blond head.
You pause underneath to light a cocktail joint
spreading your legs wide to support
the weight of the black plastic lighter you hold in your hands.
I sneak up behind you and nudge your shoulder.
You crack a joke. I'm the punch line.
We climb flights and cross landings
to reach your bed.
You fall facedown on the duvet.
I flip you over and peel back layers of clothing.
Your chest is a road map of scars —
red routes leading to your heart.
I place my hands on top of this cloverleaf.
You slip between my fingers.

Berlin

American blues play
in an after-hours club in Mitte.
You waltz alone
your feet jammed into velvet pumps
your fingers pressed against
the satin stripes that run
the length of your black wool trousers.

Beneath a plaster spiderweb
on the ceiling of your hotel/whorehouse
you kiss a blond boy's chest.
Light reflects off the stubble
of his four-day beard.
He whispers, *Ich liebe dich.*
You don't believe him.

In the morning you step
outdoors and confused for a moment
gaze up the Kurfürstendamm
and dream of an alterable world.

You

the world was a devil's curse
a daily challenge to survive
the next day of work or no work
friends or solitude
often despair
until you
sunshine and hope
the bright half of life
emotions embarrassing at first
but now as characteristic of me
as of you
to whom I have given
a lifetime of kisses
and accepted
your lifetime in exchange

For WJM

You're so happy
you blast the horn

of your bomb of a car
when you turn into the driveway

of the farmhouse
where I wait for you.

You skid to a stop
beside a pink flamingo

you planted in the lawn
the last time you were here

and walk on long legs
into the kitchen

where I stand
slouched over a porcelain countertop

buttering an English muffin.
I peer through

my morning space storm
at you grinning at me

bursting with excess energy
which you right away

put to good use
by making an omelet for us.

Outer Banks

We choose
a deserted stretch of sand

and spread our blanket.
I read Trollope

while baking brown.
You walk for miles along

the seashore and when you return
you have a deeply thought-out plan

but I know only Trollope's
overstuffed interiors

the odor of Coppertone
and the glare of the beach.

Two Titles
Borrowed from William Carlos Williams

This Is Just to Say

I cooked all the vegetables
in the refrigerator.
The ones you brought
home from the farm.
I was afraid they would spoil
if I left them untouched.
We will eat them together
when we see each other
tonight. A vegetable stew
for the 2 of us.

Marriage

So alike
these 2 men.
2 streams
flowing together
through decades of
traveling fucking
gardening bickering
& parenthood
of a couple of cats.
But a ceremony?
What would that mean?

Multiverse

There's a parallel reality
across the galaxies
where we behave better
than here.
There is no bitterness
in our partings
or false smiles
when we meet again.
We see into and through
each other in outer space.
And what else is different
in our duplicate world?
Our skin is blue
our hair is glorious
and the weather is perfect.

Next Summer

We'll ride the Cyclone
even though it makes us throw up

I'll wear my bucket hat
and you'll bring your Speedo

we'll walk down the beach
and jump into the Atlantic

you'll bury me in the sand
and I'll smile for the camera

my shoulder won't ache
and your feet won't hurt

we'll dance on the boardwalk
until the sun sets behind the projects

you'll eat cotton candy
and I'll have a hot dog

life won't be rough
next summer on Coney Island

Two-Day Bender

We started drinking gin uptown
smoking hand-rolled cigarettes
taking taxis from bar to bar.

Forty-eight hours later we walked
downtown on Second Avenue
carrying open cans of beer
bags of chips
and the Sunday *Times*.

You told me knives
stabbed you on the same walk
two years earlier.
You wanted my sympathy
but I wouldn't give it to you.

The moon was full and snow was on the ground.
It was ten degrees Fahrenheit
and I couldn't feel the cold.

Shelter

It took them years to decorate their house in Morocco

    no longer a couple
    they never moved in

Instead they rented the place to tourists

    4 flights up to the kitchen
    2 down to the bathroom

Some rooms lost and never found
A dog lost in the 3rd floor hallway

    the house a white cave on top of a hill

Tourists became confused by its eccentricities
The view from the balcony was extraordinary
but there was no reentry to the house
and to get to the street they had to swing on vines

cats became kittens
and apes overran the place
gibbons not usually encountered in that climate

    Everyone left after a few nights

Kiss-off

That one
spat in my eye for the last time.
I don't love him anymore.
Not long after he met me, he said
see you and he left the country.
He was gone so long on his voyage
I got bored and fucked someone else.
The release of orgasm made me forget
him for a while
until one day I saw that bastard
standing alone in a bar,
and he looked at me as if
he didn't know my name.
I said hello,
but he turned away.
Now I've decided to bury
myself in an occupation
other than love.
Boyfriend, I warn you,
stay away from me.
Save your mournful gaze
for some other sucker.

I Still Get Jealous

On the checkout line
at the Pathmark
I see a picture
of the man
you took up with
after you ditched the man
you left me for.

"The Sexiest Man Alive"
smiles at me
from the cover
of a magazine.

It makes me mad.

Anamnesis

My stomach
growls in the night
and disturbs
a dream.
The grandfather clock
one floor below and
two rooms removed
tolls one, two, three
o'clock in the morning.
I swallow decades in
chunks and spit out
images of you.
Church bells ring
and your face
appears like a gun
pulled from a forgotten
drawer.
A name falls
from my mouth
a word I've tried to erase
from my memory banks.
Then *you* toss in your sleep
and I rest my hand
on your shoulder.
Your blood warms me.

The Place on High Was Our Shared Mystery

Our second summer: New England light
reflected off your teeth and beard.

We walked the sands of no man's land
where only pilots spied on our lovemaking.

Your aura: I saw sunshine
and blue light reflected in your eyes.

You emanated faint warmth and an animal odor.
My hands caressed the air around your body.

Our potted plant: taller now, even stately,
it has moved from your care to another home.

Your camera: you stand behind it waving
your personality like a flag. A dialogue ensues.

Your favorite painting: I saw her today
at the Metropolitan Museum of Art.

Our songs: they have disappeared
from the jukebox.

Locations: I am stationery,
and you maintain perpetual motion.

Dead Boyfriend

You lived your life behind velvet ropes.
Your name appeared on all the lists.
I linked arms with you for several years
sometimes bathing in your golden light
sometimes getting blinded by it.

You seemed to have so much
of the stuff everyone wanted.
Even your name signified plenty.
But it was a truncated name
from a longer less evocative one.

The world chopped up our relationship
before we were ready to let go of it.
And we chose opposite coasts.
Or did we melt like an ice cream sundae
left out in the desert sun?

When you died you left so much unsaid.
Your friends and lovers tried to fill in the gaps
while talking to the author of your biography.
But the scent of you didn't get published
among the photographs and reminiscences.

You were dulce de leche.
I loved the feel of you and the way
your jeans slipped off your skinny hips.
I can still taste you and smell you
even without closing my eyes.

HIV

robbed me of all my ex-boyfriends
each death hurt like hell
the obituary
the last time scared me
so long after drug cocktails
we were all supposed to live

Our Gay Bar

The smell of it is
what I remember.
The scent of spilled beer
and semen, cigarettes, ass.

I go there too many years later
and it's a straight bar
with pool table, bartenders and toilets
in their familiar places
but sanitized, unsexed.

In the men's room
I catch a whiff of you and me
and some of the others,
odors left over from the time
when we were all still alive.

Acknowledgments

The author extends his thanks to the following publications:

Colere: A Journal of Cultural Exploration	"For M.R."
CreamDrops: An Art and Literary Journal for Gay Men	"Happy Hour," and "The Place on High Was Our Shared Mystery"
Ganymede Unfinished: A Tribute to John Stahle and His Journal Ganymede, Alexander, AR: Sibling Rivalry Press, 2010	"Open Heart Surgery," "Berlin," and "Anamnesis"
Mary: A Literary Quarterly	"Our Gay Bar"
The Q Review	"Courtship," "Ambisexuality," and "I Still Get Jealous"
Superficial Flesh	"Next Summer"
THIS Literary Magazine	"Shelter"

About the Author

Geer Austin's poetry and fiction has appeared in *Big Bridge*, *MiPOesias*, *Ganymede Unfinished*, *THIS Literary Magazine* and *Potomac Review*, among others. He is the former editor of *NYB*, a New York / Berlin arts magazine. He led creative writing workshops for many years independently and through the New York Writers Coalition, most recently at New Alternatives for LGBT Homeless Youth. He lives in New York City

A NOTE ON THE TYPE

This book is set in Minion Pro, an Old-Style serif typeface designed by Robert Slimbach of Adobe Systems, and released in 1990 by Linotype. Inspired by the mass-produced publications of the late Renaissance, but with a contemporary crispness and clarity not possible with the print machinery of that era, even by the best of the Renaissance typographers, this modern-day interpretation is well regarded for its classic baroque-rooted styling and its enhanced legibility. One of the five or six most widely used typefaces for trade paperback fiction published in the United States over the past several years, Minion Pro is the typeface adopted by the Smithsonian for its logo. The name Minion is derived from the traditional classification and nomenclature of typeface sizes; *minion,* the size between *brevier* and *nonpareil,* approximates a modern 7-point lettering size.

www.ingramcontent.com/pod-product-compliance
Lightning Source LLC
Chambersburg PA
CBHW061758040426
42447CB00011B/2361